Original title:
Island Breezes and Heartbeats

Copyright © 2025 Creative Arts Management OÜ
All rights reserved.

Author: Lila Davenport
ISBN HARDBACK: 978-1-80581-488-7
ISBN PAPERBACK: 978-1-80581-015-5
ISBN EBOOK: 978-1-80581-488-7

Embraced by Nature's Pulse

On a floating chair, I sip my drink,
With a tiny umbrella, what do you think?
The seagulls cackle like a sitcom crew,
While I wave back, feeling like a fool.

The palm trees dance like they're in a show,
Waving at me in a gentle flow.
Coconuts drop, they roll and they bop,
Joking with me, they just don't stop.

The sun's a comedian, bright with a grin,
Casting its warmth, oh where do I begin?
I slip in the waves, a splash and a splash,
Giggling like kids, like a spontaneous bash.

The tides bring laughter, the sand tickles toes,
As the ocean hums softly, nobody knows.
I chase the crab that scuttles away,
He pops his claws like, "Not today!"

So here I lounge, with laughter in air,
Nature's pulse got me dancing with flair.
Life's too short to take things with dread,
I'm just a fool with a sunburned head!

Love Amidst the Coconut Palms

Underneath the tall green trees,
A squirrel steals my lunch with ease.
I chase him while I sing out loud,
A coconut joins, crowding the crowd.

We dance like leaves in the warm, bright sun,
With laughter that echoes; oh, what fun!
The squirrels laugh too; they think they're grand,
All while I plot to snatch back my hand.

Swaying to the Saltwater Melody

The waves dance close, they splash and play,
They tickle toes in a silly way.
I leap and trip on a slimy rock,
The fish all chuckle—not a single shock!

The seagulls squawk like they own the place,
While I chase my hat—it's quite a race!
With every dive and every leap,
The ocean's laughs are oh so deep!

Close to the Whispering Surf

I built a sandcastle, tall and proud,
But a wave decided to laugh out loud.
It knocked down my tower, my royal seat,
While crabs in tuxedos danced on my feet.

The tide sings softly, a silly tune,
While I dodge a jellyfish in the afternoon.
"Oh what a mishap!" I giggle and sway,
As the tide pulls my troubles far, far away.

Embrace of the Untamed Waters

In a kayak that wiggles, I find my way,
My oar slips, and I'm dragged like play!
The fish take photos, they give a cheer,
While I paddle in circles, quite unclear.

The sun shines down, it's a glorious sight,
Except for the seagull who thinks it's a fight!
He swoops and dive-bombs, oh what a day,
I might just paddle far, far away!

Whispers of the Tides

Seagulls squawking in the morn,
Dancing seashells, brightly worn.
Crabs that march in goofy lines,
Imitating all our signs.

Waves that tickle sandy toes,
Sandcastles with wobbly rows.
A hermit crab in borrowed dress,
Complains about its lack of finesse.

Beach balls bouncing, kids in flight,
Launching into a sand-filled sight.
Kites that tumble, flapping wild,
As parents chase down their own child.

Sunburned noses, laughter's sound,
Everyone's sitting close around.
With each wave, a chuckle shared,
Tales of all the fun we dared.

Lullabies of the Shore

The tide hums lullabies so sweet,
As flip-flops dance on sandy feet.
Starfish playing peek-a-boo,
Who knew they were this shy, it's true?

A jellyfish floats in a jig,
While kids proclaim, "Look at that pig!"
It's just a seal, but who's to know?
With all this giggling, off we go!

Sunscreen slathered everywhere,
Parents look like they've no care.
Sandy snacks that crunch and munch,
Ants having their own picnic lunch.

Waves that whisper, giggles burst,
On this beach, worries are cursed.
Every grain of sand's a jest,
In this moment, we're truly blessed.

Serenade Beneath the Palms

Palm trees sway, a dance they make,
Coconuts drop like they were fake.
Fronds that tickle on a breeze,
We strike poses, joke with ease.

A wind chime sings with clinking cheer,
As lizards wait, full of sneer.
"Who dares to tread on our domain?"
We laugh, and they just wave in vain.

Pineapple hats and coconut cups,
Sipped with straws from funny ups.
Watermelons giggle, sliced so bright,
While crabs go scuttling to the right.

Giggling friends 'neath leafy shade,
Chasing sunbeams, a masquerade.
A day so bright, all grins and laughs,
In our hearts, these quirky gaffes.

Echoes of Sunlit Shores

Echoes bounce from wave to wave,
As goofy gulls come out to rave.
Footprints fill the golden sand,
Leading to a childish band.

Sandwiches stuffed with pickle dreams,
Soda pops with fizzy streams.
Kids invade with buckets fast,
While crabs consider a life to last.

Shells like treasures, who considers?
Kick off shoes, toss away glitters.
We belt out tunes, off-key and proud,
Bravely singing, drawing a crowd.

With every splash, a memory made,
Under the sun's warm golden braid.
Funny moments, forever stored,
In the laughter that we hoard.

Lighthouses of Longing

A lighthouse flickers, quite the sight,
Waves crash loudly, but don't take flight.
My heart, it dances, sways in glee,
Chasing seagulls, oh what a spree.

With a bucket of shrimp, I can't resist,
I wave to the gulls, they give me a twist.
They steal my snack, such cheery thieves,
Laughing like mad, oh how this deceives.

The rocks, they shimmer, like my bright shoes,
With crabby dancers, I sing my blues.
Fishermen chuckle at my silly prance,
While the lighthouse sighs, it's quite a romance.

So here's to the lights, aglow in the night,
Guiding my heart through humorous fright.
With every wave, there's a chuckle anew,
A dance on the dock, just me and my crew.

Sandcastle Reveries

I built a castle, tall and grand,
With seashell turrets, all by hand.
But the tide came in, oh what a plight,
My fortress crumbled, what a funny sight!

The seagulls laughed, they threw a feast,\nAt my expense,
I'm quite the beast.
A moat of laughter, forever flows,
As tourists snap pics, no one knows.

My bucket's empty, but my heart is full,
With sandy feet, oh what a pull!
A seashell crown atop my head,
The queen of laughter, never dread!

So here I sit, with toes in sand,
In this silly kingdom, oh isn't it grand?
I'll reign with joy, with pots and pans,
A castle of giggles, this is my plan!

Currents of Unspoken Love

The tide whispers softly, oh so sly,
In the coral's embrace, I can't deny.
Fishes swim round in an endless loop,
While I bubble up in this witty troupe.

A crab pinches on a daring spree,
While I try to dance, oh look at me!
My heart, a treasure, lost at sea,
As the dolphins laugh, so gallantly.

The seaweed waves, like a joke gone wrong,
As I trip and tumble, but still I'm strong.
With every splash, there's a pulse of fun,
Under the bright rays, I come undone.

The ocean's winks break the silent code,
With each playful wave, our secret road.
In this dance of waves, love's playful guise,
For laughter's the tide, it never lies.

Celestial Waves and Soft Whispers

Stars reflect on the wavy crest,
As I lean back, taking my rest.
With a comet's tail, my dreams take flight,
And giggles erupt in the soft moonlight.

A fish swam by with a wink so sly,
I swear it chuckled as it glided by.
In this cosmic pool, where laughter beams,
I float on dreams, or so it seems.

The moon blushed pink, while I sipped tea,
With waves of humor washing over me.
Starfish stars bidding me adieu,
As I frolic around, just me and my crew.

At dawn's first light, I prance and sway,
In this whimsical world, come what may.
The universe whispers in joyful tones,
As the waves draw laughter, far from phones.

Currents of Unspoken Yearning

A crab danced in the sand, quite spry,
His sideways moves made dolphins sigh.
Seagulls squawked with a witty jest,
While beachgoers sought the coolest rest.

A picnic blanket, oh what a snare,
Entangled with the dog's wild hair.
The sunscreen bottle, a slippery foe,
Made slipping and sliding a real show!

Children giggled, building a moat,
While dad tried to float on a pink inflatable goat.
Each wave brought laughter, a splash, a cheer,
As we dodged seagulls that swooped near.

As twilight painted the sky bright,
We toasted marshmallows by soft moonlight.
With goofy grins and a smile so wide,
We embraced the joy on this wild ride.

Shoreline Reveries

A fish with a grin swam by my toes,
Thinking my feet were a snack, goodness knows!
Kites looped and twirled in the summer sun,
While I tried to catch one, what a run!

The sandcastle wizard proclaimed his reign,
With a bucket for armor, he laughed in vain.
Laughter erupted, the tide drew near,
Devouring his fortress with waves of cheer.

Grumpy old seagull claimed my fry,
With a deft little hop, oh, my oh my!
The beachside musician strummed out a tune,
While I danced like a fool to the tune of the moon.

Under the stars, we shared silly tales,
Our laughter rolling like the sea gale.
As we packed up chips and all our fun,
The shoreline echoed, but the day was done.

Windswept Soliloquies

A hat flew off, and oh what glee,
Chasing it down, I was quite a sight to see!
The breeze was cheeky, pulling my hair,
As if it teased me without a care.

Shells whispered secrets of days gone by,
While I wondered if they'd let me try.
"Dear heart," I said, "don't let me trip!"
But the wind giggled, I fell with a flip!

Umbrellas danced like clowns in the sun,
As laughter spilled out and rolled, oh what fun!
I swore the tide winked with playful intent,
Inviting me closer with each wave's bent.

In that moment, balance quite askew,
Life felt a circus, bright and askew.
Where each heartbeat was matched with each wave,
I reveled in folly—the foolish, the brave.

Palms, Waves, and Warmth

Palms swayed low, battling a breeze,
While I danced like a leaf, aimless with ease.
The sun sprawled out on my tired back,
As I gobbled up chips, no thought of a snack.

Waves whispered stories of treasure and mirth,
But all that I found was the soft warm earth.
A fish in a bucket, a grin full of cheer,
Left me pondering what else was near.

I chuckled at crabs doing a conga line,
While chasing a rogue kite that dared to decline.
Shadows grew long as we rolled in the sand,
Spilling laughter and songs, a bond so unplanned.

At dusk we toasted, the day felt just right,
With marshmallows melting in the fading light.
All worries drifted like ships on the tide,
In this realm of sunshine, love and joy abide.

Rhythms in the Salt Air

Seagulls dance, they steal my fries,
I watch them swoop, oh how they rise!
With every bite, they squawk and dive,
Who knew my meal was so alive?

Waves clap hands upon the shore,
A silly tune, I can't ignore.
My toes are buried in warm sand,
Can life be better? Oh, it's grand!

Children laugh and slip and slide,
While sandy dogs fetch with pride.
I try to join, but lose my flip,
Falling over, what a trip!

The sun is bright, the drinks are cold,
A perfect day, or so I'm told.
Yet all my plans, they seem to stray,
I think I'll just nap the day away!

Heartstrings Tied to the Coast

Turtles sunbathe with gentle grace,
While I search for my lost shoelace.
The sand's too hot beneath my feet,
A little dance? Well, that's my beat!

A crab sidles up, with quite a stance,
I mimic it, we share a glance.
He scuttles off, I strut in place,
Wondering now, who won this race?

Kites above swirl, bright and bold,
While I drop snacks I meant to hold.
The wind's a prankster, full of glee,
It tosses treats from me to thee!

As sun dips down, I wave goodbye,
With salty hair and a weary sigh.
Yet I can't wait for the next sea spree,
To dance again, just my crab and me!

Memories in the Mist

Morning fog wraps the shoreline tight,
Where did my sunglasses take flight?
I glance around, but all seems lost,
Or maybe I just need to toss!

Shells whisper tales of ocean lore,
As I chase them, as they soar.
Caught in a wave, they splash away,
I stand there laughing, what a display!

A dolphin leaps, a fishy grin,
And I try to mimic, thus begins!
But all my splashes make me wet,
Another prank I'll not forget!

As evening falls, the stars ignite,
I trip on sand, oh what a sight!
Yet as I laugh, I've grown to see,
The joy in chaos, just let it be!

Swaying with the Wind

Palm trees swaying, you're quite the show,
Don't look at me, I'm just below!
My drink spills while I try to cheer,
Oh, what a dance, it's off the rear!

A pirate's hat blows past my head,
I chase it down, well, that's my thread.
With laughter ringing, shadows play,
At night, the stars join in the fray!

Drink umbrellas twist in gusty glee,
As I try juggling—oh dear me!
A seagull scolds my poor finesse,
Perhaps I should just take a rest!

But as I spin, the world spins too,
A silly whirl of ocean blue.
With friends around and laughter near,
I'll take the tumble, shed no tear!

Tides of Embrace

In flip-flops racing, they tumble down,
Sandy toes giggling in this beachy town.
Seagulls squawk, stealing fries in flight,
While sunscreen battles the sun's delight.

Shells are treasures, but oh what a mess,
Digging for gold leads to sticky excess.
Someone's lost their hat in the wild sea dance,
It's a comical chase, oh what a chance!

Lullabies of the Ocean Spray

The wave's a lullaby, will it rock me sweet?
But splashes and laughter make it hard to sleep.
A crab wearing shades scuttles past with style,
While sunburned tourists rest, looking like a pile.

Fish leap for joy, trying to steal a show,
As swimmers flail, doing the 'I don't know.'
The tide rolls in, with a chuckle so grand,
Life's a splash zone, come take a stand!

Secrets Carried by the Zephyr

Whispers of wind tease the palm trees high,
While beach balls travel with a carefree sigh.
A conch shell confesses its secrets in jest,
As we sip on drinks with umbrellas, impressed.

But watch out for gulls, they're plotting a raid,
Scavenging snacks that you've carelessly laid.
They swoop and they dive, oh what a ruckus,
Laughing as they triumph—those feathery rascals!

Waves of the Heart's Murmur

The tide pulls and tugs like a playful friend,
While beachgoers try not to slip at the bend.
With sun-kissed laughter and frothy delight,
We dance on the shore till it's dark as night.

But here comes a wave, oh what a surprise!
It drenches our picnic; water fills our eyes.
We laugh as we soak, forgetting the care,
Life's a splashy venture, let's just be aware!

Tides of Forgotten Passion

Waves tickle toes in the sun,
Seagulls squawk, oh what fun!
A crab scuttles, quick and spry,
Dodging shadows, oh my, oh my!

A beach ball flies with daring fate,
Lands on a sunbather's plate.
'Hey, I ordered fries, not this mess!'
The beach crew laughs, what a success!

Sandcastle dreams, a mighty dive,
But the tide whispers, 'Can't survive!'
Moats fill up, and there goes the throne,
Muffled giggles as they're overthrown.

With beach hats tipped and tan lines bold,
They reminisce tales hilariously told.
The ocean giggles softly, it seems,
As laughter reigns in sunlit dreams.

Emotions Painted in Seafoam

Coconut drinks with tiny umbrellas,
Sip them slow, avoid the yellers.
Oh! A wave just took my chair,
Saltwater splatters sprinkle my hair!

Dancing crabs in a one-man show,
Twisting and turning—a funny flow.
While sunburned tourists chase them down,
'Hey buddy, you can't wear that crown!'

Waves roll in with a teasing grin,
With every splash, they pull us in.
We trip and tumble, causing great cheer,
'Water ballet? More like water beer!'

Seagulls cackle, plotting their feast,
As someone tosses lunch, oh what a beast!
Sandy sandwiches, now a delight,
Watching the chaos from morning till night.

The Dance of Light and Shadows

'Look at me!' a shadow said,
As it danced around my head.
I waved back, trying to be smooth,
But tripped on my flip-flops, lost my groove!

Palm trees sway in the warm, sweet air,
Like they're grooving without a care.
A flock of birds, doing the conga,
While I'm stuck doing the awkward bongo.

Sunset paints the sky with flair,
While sunburn lingered, I had no care.
Laughter echoes over the tide,
As my friends all roll, trying to hide.

But alas, as night wraps its shawl,
The shadows gathered, having a ball.
One made a joke—can't quite recall,
Telling stories that made our cheeks sprawl!

Secrets Held in Sandy Grains

Whispers of grains underfoot,
Tell tales of a silly pursuit.
Each shuffle and squish, a secret shared,
While I wonder if my flip-flops fared.

A treasure hunt for lost things bright,
They say a seashell contains pure delight.
I found a sock! Is this my prize?
The laughter erupts, oh what a surprise!

Mermaids sing and sirens call,
But all I've got is a sunburned pall.
Jellyfish fashion show in mid-dip,
I slip and slide, it's quite a trip.

Under the moon, we make our plans,
To count the stars, hold sweaty hands.
With every giggle, our worries unwind,
In this carnival of joy, we're all intertwined.

Poetry of Sandy Toes and Salty Air

In flip-flops I stumble, like a clown,
With grains of sand stuck to my frown.
Seagulls squawk like they own the place,
While I flee from a crab with a scuttling pace.

The sun's a joker, it's playing tricks,
Melting ice cream with sunburned licks.
Waves giggle, tickling my weary feet,
As I shuffle away from that jellyfish seat.

Finding seashells, oh what a delight,
Except for that one, it gave me a fright.
It's a rock, not a treasure, what a letdown!
I'll bury my woes in the sandy ground.

But oh! The laughter, it fills the air,
From friends in the surf, without a care.
Even the tide seems to chuckle and tease,
In this goofy paradise, I'm eager to please.

Laughter in the Wind's Caress

The breeze blew in with a snicker and grin,
Tugging my hat as I tossed it in.
With hair like seaweed, a sight to behold,
Each gust's a prankster, daring and bold.

The palm trees dance, wearing leafy crowns,
As I trip on a flip-flop; I'm falling down.
A crab joins the fun, with a sidestep flair,
Pinching my toe—oh, that's not fair!

A kite swoops low with a cheeky dive,
Draws in my sandwich, oh, how it thrives!
Eating my lunch, while I just stand and stare,
The sky's a comedian, no one can compare.

Bubbles float up, giggling in the sky,
With seagulls laughing as they swoop by.
Life's a funny play, with jokes to share,
In every whirl of the ocean air.

Hearts Singing with the Tide

Waves flirt with rocks, it's quite a show,
They splash and jest, and put on a flow.
With shells as their audience, they break into song,
It's a quirky concert; can't help but sing along.

At sunset, the sky (oh, what a rude tease!)
Paints itself rosy like a clown at ease.
While fish wave hello with their giddy glee,
Each splash a reminder that fun's always free.

In the distance, a buoy's tut-tutting away,
As if to say, "Hey, stay here and play!"
Even the dolphins join in with a flip,
Creating a whirlpool, each twist a funny trip.

With hearts like confetti, we dance by the shore,
Silly tunes echo, who could ask for more?
The tide has a rhythm, a beat of its own,
In this watery playground, we've truly grown.

Tranquility Wrapped in Ocean's Embrace

A hammock swings low, held by trees so wise,
As I snooze in the sun, dreaming of fries.
The sound of the surf is a lullaby prank,
While a crab steals my chips—I guess it's a tank!

In the distance, a dog starts to bark,
Chasing away shadows, igniting a spark.
With a flip of its tail, it catches the wave,
A salty doggo, oh, how it misbehaves!

My sunburn's a badge, I wear it with pride,
Like a lobster in sunglasses, I cannot hide.
The sunscreen's made friends with my sandy toes,
They laugh and they dance like a pair of best bros.

Under the palm trees, we giggle and sigh,
Life's a funny movie that whizzes on by.
In this tranquil chaos, we find our grace,
Wrapped in this laughter, this warm, silly space.

Heartstrings Tethered to the Coast

On sandy shores we dance around,
With flip-flops flying, laughter's found.
A crab waves near, looking bemused,
While seagulls squawk, quite confused.

The sunburned nose, a badge of pride,
We chase the waves, like kids we hide.
Palm trees sway, they gossip and grin,
As beach balls bounce, let the fun begin.

Shells line the sand, a treasure hunt,
But watch your step, or you'll face a stunt.
With each splash from a rogue wave's jest,
We chuckle loud, forgetting rest.

Even the tides have jokes to share,
As jellyfish float, without a care.
We become sea creatures, wild and free,
This wacky ocean life, just you and me.

Serenade of the Restless Sea

The waves roll in with a silly cheer,
Spitting foam like a sea dog's sneer.
We build our castles, a soggy delight,
Only for them to disappear in the night.

A fish jumps high, wearing a hat,
While dolphins giggle, imagine that!
The salty spray, a face full of fun,
Who knew the sea was such a pun?

Seagulls swoop, stealing my fries,
While we're out here cracking wise.
With every splash comes a silly song,
In this carefree world, we all belong.

As sunset paints the sky with flair,
We wave at the sun, a giant glare.
With laughter rippling, we'll never cease,
To find the humor, that's our peace.

Harmonies of Driftwood and Dreams

Two sticks make music, as crabs tap dance,
We join the rhythm, caught in a trance.
With driftwood brushes, we paint the night,
Our laughter ringing, pure delight.

Twirling under stars, we take our chance,
Waves join in on our wild prance.
A conch shell serenades our quest,
It's a party where crabs are the best.

The moon plays tricks, casts shadows in glee,
While we trip over roots like a comedy spree.
With each misstep, we're howling loud,
No better audience than the waves, so proud.

With hearts so full, we muddle our way,
In this sandy wonder where we'll always play.
As driftwood whispers, "Life's a grand show,"
We bow to the tides for the laughs we know.

Loving the Whispering Winds

The breeze comes in, a cheeky tease,
Messing with hair, it does as it please.
With every gust, a giggle ensues,
As hats go flying, you'll hear the news!

The wind howls tales, spins stories in flight,
Of fish that flash in the pale moonlight.
We chase down laughter on this carefree ride,
With salty kisses, the ocean's pride.

Each puff full of mischief, every turn a smile,
We ride the gales, let's stay a while.
As the sun dips low, colors collide,
With winds as our witness, we'll never hide.

So here's to the breezes that bring us delight,
In this world of whimsy, we'll dance through the night.
With every heartbeat, we'll laugh and we'll sing,
For life's just a party on the wings of spring.

Charm of the Sunlit Brine

The seagulls caw, they steal my fries,
With salty wings they sneak and fly.
I wave my arms, they make me dance,
To steal my lunch, they're in a trance.

The waves whisper jokes, full of mirth,
As I trip over the sand, for what it's worth.
"Sir, your hat is now in the sea!"
Well, it's better off without me, you see.

A crab in a tux, how absurdly grand,
He pinches my toe, then runs on the sand.
With laughter that bubbles like foam on the shore,
I guffaw at nature, wanting more!

Oh sun, you tickle, you warm my back,
While I awkwardly dance, it's quite a knack.
In this comedic play of sun and sea,
Life is a farce, and I'm the marquee!

Melodies of the Tidal Dance

The waves clap hands, a rhythmic beat,
As I twirl and stumble on my two left feet.
Starfish chuckle from their rocky chairs,
While seaweed sways, none of it cares.

A dolphin jumps with a gleeful splash,
I try to dance, but trip in a crash.
The fish form a band, they play my tune,
With bubbles that burst, a comical boon.

The crabs tap dance in a shiny line,
I join them too, though I'm far from fine.
They pinch my bum, and oh, what a stir,
I bow in gratitude, much to their blur.

In the salty air filled with laughter and fun,
I waddle my way, under the sun.
Yet as the tide rolls back, they disperse in a glance,
Leaving me wondering: was it a dance?

Solace in the Gentle Surf

Gentle waves lap like a fleeting tickle,
I chuckle as clams perform a quick wiggle.
With a sunhat too big, I make quite a scene,
As I sip my coconut, feeling like a queen.

The tides tease my toes with a smirk and a splash,
"Catch me if you can!" they bubble and dash.
I chase the foam, but it leads me astray,
Into a shower of water—oh, what a spray!

A sandcastle stands, proud and so tall,
Then a rogue wave decides it's a ball.
"Not my fortress!" I squeal, but it's too late,
As the tides laugh and decide my fate.

But in the silliness of this lively shore,
I find joy in chaos, and I crave more!
With salty air and laughter that's light,
The world feels right under the sun so bright.

Caresses of the Warm Current

The sun tickles my back as I float,
A sea turtle swims by wearing a coat.
"Fancy meeting you," I wave with glee,
He flicks his flipper like, "Try to keep up with me!"

I ride the waves like a small little cork,
Until a rogue splash makes my face look like a fork.
Giggles erupt from the fishes below,
"Look at the human, he's quite the show!"

With every crash, my worries dissolve,
In the foamy embrace, I revolve and evolve.
The sun makes the water a sparkling swirl,
While I attempt to perfect my churlish whirl.

So here on the seas, where laughs are the best,
I'll dance with the currents, a perpetual jest.
In this swirling splash, I'll always stay free,
A clown in the waves, just my cup of tea!

Heartfelt Whispers Beneath the Palm

In a hammock made of dreams, I sway,
With a coconut drink, I shout hooray!
The parrots laugh as they fly by,
While I pretend to be very spry.

Sunshine tickles my nose so bright,
As I chase my sandals in playful flight.
The sea turtle winks from the sea,
Saying, "Chill out, just be free!"

A crab scuttles by with a quirky grin,
I toss him a chip, hoping to win.
He does a dance, oh what a show!
While I just sit and eat my dough.

The palm leaves rustle, giggles all around,
With every gust, pure joy is found.
If laughter could float, it surely would,
Riding the waves, just like it should.

Harmonies of the Seafoam Dance

The waves break in rhythm, a goofy beat,
As two seagulls try to snag a treat.
They squawk and flail, what a sight to see,
Like dancers in love, so wild and free.

Surfboards glide with the style of a cat,
Each wipe-out paired with a splashing spat.
The lifeguard giggles, looks quite absurd,
As he calls out, 'Don't swim with the herd!'

A jellyfish floats, wearing a crown,
With colors so bright, it could win a gown.
But if you touch, oh the electric sting,
You'll dance away fast, like a silly spring!

Even the sun seems to roll its rays,
With tiny sparkles caught in sunlit plays.
A floatie parade, all colors galore,
Laughing together, who could ask for more?

Heartbeats Nestled in Sunbeams

I lay on the sand, my heart is a drum,
The waves sing along, oh what a hum!
My napkin flaps like a flag of peace,
While seagulls launch into bright aerial fleece.

A beach ball rolls, oh where will it go?
Chasing after it is quite the show.
It bounces and wiggles, a playful tease,
While sunscreen globs land in the breeze.

Sandcastles rise with great aspirations,
But a wave comes crashing, oh the frustrations!
Some shells make faces, quite the array,
As I scratch my head, "What's gone astray?"

Laughter erupts as the children compete,
Building the silliest structure to beat.
With each tiny wave, full of glee,
We dance on the shore, just you and me.

The Tide's Romantic Revelation

The moon hangs low, like a grinning cat,
While waves whisper secrets, imagine that!
Shells play Cupid, aiming for hearts,
Creating a rhythm where love never departs.

In the moonlight glow, the crabs put on shoes,
Tap-dancing together in colorful hues.
Their tiny pinches, like flirty peeks,
As they giggle about how everyone sneaks.

The breeze carries tales, twists, and spins,
Of two dolphins competing in watery grins.
With each leap they take, it's quite absurd,
As the audience howls, 'Did you see that bird?'

As twilight descends, a serenade's near,
With laughter and joy, we toast with cheer.
For love is a dance, with waves as the floor,
In this playful world, who could want more?

Murmurs of the Surfing Waves

The ocean's giggle in the sun,
Splashing water, just for fun.
Seagulls laugh like brats on a spree,
Dancing around like they own the sea.

Surfboards wobble, riders fall,
Splashing like fish at the beach ball.
A flip, a twist—they're out of control,
The tide's a jester, it plays its role.

Sunburned noses and sandy toes,
While sun hats fly in the ocean's blows.
Everyone's grinning, sun-kissed faces,
Chasing seashells and making 'fun' places.

So come take a dip in this chaos here,
Where laughter echoes and brings good cheer.
Beneath the surf, we shout and yell,
In this watery world, all is well.

Gentle Winds of the Solstice

The wind tickles like a feathered tease,
Rustling through palms with the greatest of ease.
Laughter swirls with each playful gust,
Whispers of secrets, in breezes we trust.

Flip-flops fly as we run with glee,
Chasing each other like kids by the sea.
"Catch me if you can," a shouted dare,
As sandy toes dance through the salty air.

Picnic blankets take off, a sight to behold,
Chips and dip fly like stories retold.
Kites dance around, a mischievous game,
While we yell back, "Hey, it's not the same!"

The evening wraps up like a warm hug,
Under a sky that starts to unplug.
With giggles still lingering, we dream and sleep,
In the embrace of the night, we giggle and peep.

Lanterns of the Night Sky

Stars twinkle like winking eyes,
As we lay beneath the vast, dark skies.
Lanterns sway like they're telling tales,
Of whimsical journeys, and far-off trails.

The moon plays tricks, a glow on my nose,
As if it's laughing at our silly rows.
We try to catch shadows that dance on our face,
In this quirky game, there's no need for grace.

Fireflies flicker like tiny bulbs bright,
Their giggles mix with the cool, breezy night.
Jumping for joy, the kids take a spin,
Spinning like tops—let the fun begin!

As lanterns light up, like wishes on strings,
We gather around for the laughter it brings.
In this silly show, our hearts intertwine,
With moments like these, oh how we shine!

Solitary Starlit Serenades

Alone in the night, singing off-key,
With crickets providing the harmony.
The moon is my backup, just rolling its beams,
As I perform solo, lost in my dreams.

The stars join me in twinkling applause,
With laughter and joy, they take a pause.
"Is that a song, or a duck getting choked?"
Even the night sky with giggles is cloaked.

I trip on the sand, my serenade breaks,
While the waves just roll, making rippling lakes.
The wind joins the chorus, a wild, funny tune,
Swaying those palm trees, all under the moon.

So let's sing together, let voices be free,
Under these starlights, just you and me.
With chuckles and chuckles that never cease,
In this silly serenade, we find our peace.

Embracing the Serene Waves

I danced with waves that splashed my toes,
A crab in the sand wore fancy clothes.
Seagulls swooped down, a raucous choir,
Catching my snacks, oh, I never tire!

Flip-flops squeaked in a silly tune,
Chasing my hat like a playful loon.
The sun was a joker, bright and bold,
It winked at my laughter, tales untold.

A coconut fell, a clonk on my head,
I laughed like a kid, 'oh dear' I said.
My drink took a tumble, splashed on my lap,
A cocktail inside a messy trap!

With every wave, I found pure glee,
Nature's sheer joy, a wacky spree.
The ocean's embrace, so cool and wide,
With giggles and grins, let's enjoy the ride!

Solitude and the Gentle Wind

The breeze whispers secrets, just for me,
Teasing my hair like a playful spree.
A lonely palm sways, just one in a row,
Wondering if it's got friends to show.

I asked a fish for a chat, it just swam,
No jokes, no puns, simply a sham.
A sunburned lobster struts with great flair,
Telling all tales of life unaware.

A flip-flop's gone rogue, it leaps and it jumps,
While I try to catch it, tripping on lumps.
Oh gentle wind, you laugh at my plight,
With a cheeky poke, you disappear from sight!

I sip on my drink, it's gone in a flash,
A hummingbird's feast, it's quite the bash.
Alone but not lonely in whims that I spin,
The world's such a nutty, delightful din!

The Pulse of Distant Shores

From rocky coastlines to soft sandy beds,
I chased down the pings of surf with my spreads.
Each wave that crashed sang a cheeky song,
"Do a jig!" said the tide, "You can't go wrong!"

A jellyfish boogied, it shimmied on by,
I laughed so hard, I could almost fly.
A gull squawked a tune, misplaced in the breeze,
Swapping my playlist with raspberries and tease.

An octopus winked from beneath a sea shell,
Its dance moves enchanted, it cast quite a spell.
I tried to join in, but tangled my feet,
"Flip with me, buddy!" but slipped on my seat.

The rhythm of tides felt like pure fate,
"Let loose!" shouted friends, "Don't overinflate!"
With laughter in waves and the sun on my face,
I found my groove, embraced the wild space!

Kisses from the Tropical Skies

In the land where the sun gives cheeky pecks,
Palm trees wave 'hi' with their own little flex.
A cloud tried to nap, but fell on my head,
Mumbling sweet dreams, "Oh, you're too well-fed!"

The rain danced a tango, embraced all around,
Bouncing off rooftops, a bubbly sound.
Each drop brought a chuckle, quite unexpected,
Telling me stories of vacation-deflected.

A parrot cracked jokes while perched on the line,
"Mangoes are sweeter when sippin' on brine!"
I laughed till I cried at this tropical charm,
Nature's own humor, its own kind of balm.

With each fleeting sunset, my heart would race,
If laughter's a treasure, I've found the right place.
So here in the tropics, with joy I shall rise,
I'm kissed by the dawn and the colorful skies!

Dance of the Coral Veil

Beneath the waves, the fish wear shoes,
They twist and twirl, they sing the blues.
A crab with a hat starts to prance,
Who knew sea life could lead a dance?

The seahorse spins, oh what a sight,
Doing the limbo, holding on tight.
A dolphin laughs, the seaweed sways,
As clams clap shells to the music's plays.

A starfish tries to steal the show,
But has two left feet—oh, what a woe!
Yet everyone joins with a giggly cheer,
Underwater parties, give a big cheer!

With sea cucumbers busting a move,
It's a coral ball, let's all groove.
Unusual friends who can't help but sway,
When the tide brings laughter, come out and play.

Hearts Adrift in Sunshine

A lazy seagull steals my fries,
While I just sit and aim for skies.
With sunblock splattered on my nose,
I wave at fish in their fin suits, who knows?

The sandcastles look a bit off beat,
Squinting in sun, they look quite neat.
The crabs wear shells, each fashionably bold,
While turtles all wear shades, oh so sold!

A beach ball bounces, it lands with a thud,
Right on the head of a slipping dud.
We all burst out in a fit of glee,
When tides of laughter wash over me.

With ice cream dripping down my chin,
And all my friends, let the fun begin!
For nothing quite beats a day like this,
Under the sun, with nothing amiss.

The Promise of Endless Shores

In a boat made of coconut shells,
We sail on dreams, where laughter dwells.
The captain's a parrot, squawking away,
Claiming he's found the treasure day by day.

The compass spins, the maps are skewed,
While jellybeans fill the captain's food.
"Off course," he shrieks, "by two whole miles!"
But nothing can ruin our joy-filled trials.

We pitch a tent for a sandwich feast,
As mosquitoes join, each craving a beast.
But still we munch on our floppy bread,
With smiles that brighten even the dead.

So here we float on this salty tide,
With winds of whimsy forever our guide.
Shall we drift forever as laughter soars?
For there's treasure aplenty on these endless shores!

Dreams Cradled by Gentle Currents

A hammock hangs from palm trees tall,
Where I kick back and feel so small.
The roosters ruckus with every crow,
Dancing in dreams to a rhythm they know.

I sway to whispers from the ocean deep,
Where wishes are made, and mermaids leap.
The starry night spins tales of delight,
With fish in bow ties, oh what a sight!

I snooze away, wrapped in the breeze,
While crabs review their comedy keys.
They laugh about jokes washed ashore,
Like soggy pages from tales of yore.

But morning comes with a giggling squawk,
As all the creatures join in to talk.
And in this place, where mirth never ends,
I find my heart and dance with my friends.

Where Love Meets the Seafoam

In a world where flippers dance,
And crabs wear shades with style,
We laugh as the sea takes a chance,
Falling over in a wave, quite vile.

Fish are gossiping in the tide,
Whales queue up for a selfie,
With seaweed skirts, they take great pride,
While flipping fins, they say, 'Oh me!'.

A dolphin's flip, a joyful splash,
As seagulls dive for fries, oh dear!
Amidst the foam, our hearts clash,
In love's comedy, let's cheer!

We build sandcastles tall and proud,
Until the tide takes them away,
"Look out!" we yell, our giggles loud,
As sea creatures join our play.

Sunsets Adrift on Gentle Waves

As the sun dips low, we hold our breath,
While pirates toast with coconut cups,
A parrot squawks, 'You'll meet your death!'
But really, it just wants our snacks, what's up?

Waves tickle toes, a slippery dance,
As we chase jellyfish, quite absurd,
They wink and wave in a gooey trance,
'Join us!' they giggle, 'Have you heard?'

The horizon's blush begins to glow,
While crabs go speed-dating on the sand,
We wave long to sunken treasure below,
Mysteries await, but we just have to stand!

And laughter fills the salty air,
As seagulls dive-bomb for our fries,
We catch our dreams, with not a care,
In this world of giggles and surprise.

Ocean's Embrace

Beneath a hat that's far too wide,
We splash and dive without a care,
Fish swim by with a wink and glide,
While dolphins tease with salty air.

A crab steals shoes and sprints away,
While we play tag with jellybeans,
Amidst the sea, we laugh and sway,
Making friends with seaweed queens.

In waves that dance, we find our groove,
Twirling past octopi in a race,
As sea turtles ask, 'Hey, do you move?'
In this wild place, we find our pace.

Together we surf the tides of fun,
With sea lions barking our song,
In this embrace, we've hardly begun,
With each belly laugh, we belong.

Serene Life at Water's Edge

At water's edge, where giggles thrive,
Crabs are busy in a comical run,
Seashells gossip, 'Do you feel alive?'
While waves give each shore a cheeky pun.

Sunbathers lounge like seals on rocks,
While seagulls plot their next bread heist,
Flip-flops sing, like playful flocks,
In the sunlit world, we're all enticed.

With laughter loud, we chase the tide,
Splashing fun, our worries drown,
Mermaids wink and swim with pride,
While we chase waves, never frown.

A beach ball bounces, quite absurd,
As laughter echoes off the sand,
In this serene life, we've all concurred,
The ocean's our playground, nothing planned.

Beneath the Canopy of Stars

The stars are winking with delight,
Yet the crabs are having a dance-off tonight.
I trip on my flip-flops, they scuttle away,
As if they own this crazy cabaret.

The moon's laughing with a silver grin,
While fish splatter paint, as they spin.
I'm trying to catch a night breeze, oh dear!
But it seems they've hired a fishy puppeteer.

The seaweed sings sweet lullabies,
To mermaids who twirl with seafoam ties.
My worries float on a buoyant thread,
All while a seagull declares me misled.

So let's lay back under twinkling lights,
With jellyfish doing their late-night flights.
I'll sip from a coconut, all warm and round,
And giggle with joy as the waves dance around.

A Breath of Warmth Among the Reefs

A blowfish puffing, looking so grand,
Winks at the clownfish in their own band.
I'm blown away by the sea's humor,
As octopuses juggle, just a real bloomer.

I dove too deep, lost my cool,
While snorkeling past the coral school.
Tropical fish snicker, darting about,
As I try to act calm, though inside I pout.

The sea cucumber rolls its big eyes,
While a parrotfish mocks my splashy surprise.
I'm in the splash zone of a whale's mighty tail,
Laughing so hard, I forget to exhale.

So let's breathe in the silliness, soak it in,
Dance with the dolphins, twirl and spin.
Embrace the warmth, let laughter be free,
In a world of silly splashes, just you and me.

Nautical Notes of Sweet Surrender

A boat bell rings like a silly chime,
As sailors argue over the best snack time.
With sandwiches flying, laughter's a must,
Someone yells, "It's not just my crust!"

The dolphins dive, playing peek-a-boo,
While I'm trying to steer, what's a captain to do?
The compass spins, making me dizzy,
My map's gone missing, this isn't a whizzy!

The wind whispers secrets through the sails,
While jellyfish gossip about sea snails.
My crew is knotted in ropes and giggles,
As fish swim by, doing their silly wiggles.

So let's ride the waves, churn up a storm,
With laughter and snacks, our hearts will warm.
The ocean sings us sweet tunes of glee,
In a voyage of chaos, just you and me.

Kaleidoscope of Horizon Hues

The sun dips low, painting the sky,
With colors so vivid, they make eagles cry.
I chase a rainbow on my trusty raft,
Only to find it's just a clever craft.

The gulls squawk jokes, with beaks all aglow,
As crabs in tuxedos put on a show.
I slip on wet rocks, but oh what a scene,
As the snails cheer on, "Look at that queen!"

The sunset's a clown, throws colors around,
With splashes of pink in a swirling playground.
A group of sea stars hold a dance-off at dusk,
While I laugh in delight, still smelling like musk.

So let's bask in this blend of mischief and light,
Create our own magic, from morning to night.
As hues whirl around us like laughter in pools,
We'll sail through the chaos, defying the rules.

Breeze-kissed Emotions

A sneeze from the sea, oh what a sight,
It blew my hat clean off, took flight!
Crabs side-step dance, in their own parade,
While seagulls are judging, all unafraid.

The flip-flops squeak, a comedic sound,
As I trip and tumble, fall to the ground.
Laughter spills out like waves on the shore,
Who knew that sand could be such a chore?

My drink just toppled, it's a coconut mess,
But I'll laugh it off, I must confess.
With every chuckle, the sun's getting low,
Time for a nap on the sand, oh so slow.

So here's to the giggles that life can inspire,
In a world where the humidity's higher.
With friends all around and jokes that we weave,
The day may be silly, but oh, how we believe!

Heartbeats in the Salt Air

The gulls are squawking, a raucous choir,
While I'm trying to eat, my lunch caught in fire!
Fish tacos fly, like a culinary sport,
Dinner's alive, it has other thoughts of transport!

A splash from the waves, what could it be?
A splash zone warning missing from me.
But laughter erupts like the tide on the rocks,
As I dodge the wet dog, in flip-flop stocks!

A crab called Carl wants to join our game,
He's got better moves, it's totally lame.
We're dancing together, oh what a sight,
Salt air tickles, and spirits take flight.

Our picnic's a party, a feast on the sand,
With sandwiches spinning, a whimsical band.
Hearts are all racing, with joy in the air,
In goofy mischief, we haven't a care!

Song of the Distant Horizon

Oh, wave after wave, they're singing to me,
But the rhythm's a joke, it's silly, you see!
As I try to clap, and my hands turn to bread,
The gulls roll their eyes— I just shake my head!

The sun is a DJ, spinning bright rays,
While puddles of water show off their ballet.
As I slip in a puddle, I can't help but grin,
Nature's own comedy—it's where we begin!

Flip-flops are flinging like confetti in flight,
My friend made a splash, what a laugh, what a sight!
Between naps and guffaws, the world feels so right,
We'll dance to the sunset, our spirits in flight.

It's a tune made of smiles that we'll never forget,
With joyous absurdity, we're not done yet!
Anchored in laughter, with joys to explore,
The distant horizon calls us for more!

Currents of Affection

Swirls of sea foam, a whimsical dance,
Our jokes intertwine in a tidal romance.
With a wink and a nod, we prank-tested the tide,
I wore a seaweed crown, laughing with pride!

The sun's like a comedian, brightening the day,
While friends throw sandcastles in laughable sway.
We cheer for the waves, but they have their own plans,
As they crash in our laughter and whisk away cans!

A beach ball mishap, it landed on me,
With far too much gusto, it was wild and free!
I'll deny my ballet in sand-soaked disgrace,
But the wave that followed blessed me with grace!

So here's to the folly and fun that we find,
In the joyous chaos, our hearts all aligned.
With bubbles and giggles that dance on the shore,
Together we cherish these moments and more!

Oceanic EMbliss

The waves tickle toes on the shore,
Seagulls squawk loudly, who could ask for more?
Flip-flops thrown in a splashing spree,
Dance with the tides, oh so carefree.

Surfboards wobbly, a cat on a log,
Caught in a wave, like a confused frog!
Laughter erupts as we tumble and splash,
Life's breezes entice with a jubilant crash.

Sandcastles crumble, our skills are so poor,
While beach balls soar like they've wings to explore.
Sunscreen applied, but it's a slippery mess,
And now I'm the lobster in this giant dress!

With a drink in my hand and a grin on my face,
I revel in fun at this sun-soaked place.
Who knew salty air could call forth such glee?
Oh what a life, with both laughter and tea!

Gentle Undercurrents of Love

Two crabs scuttle, oh what a sight,
Dancing together in their own little plight.
I tried to sweep you off your sandy feet,
But you dodged my advances, how rude, how sweet!

The ocean whispers secrets to the moon,
While jellyfish jiggle like they're in a tune.
You tossed me a shell, oh what a ruse,
Instead of a ring, it's a smushed-up muse!

As we chase the waves, I stumble a bit,
You laugh, and I roll, now isn't this it?
Surfboards collide, in a flurry we play,
You're yelling my name, "Come back, what'd you say?"

So let's build a driftwood palisade tall,
Where laughter echoes through the ocean's call.
With each playful push, and every silly shove,
We'll ride on the currents, all fun, all love!

Sighs of the Ocean Breeze

The sea breeze giggles, it's ticklish and wild,
Like a toddler playing, or a mischievous child.
It pulls at my hair, makes my hat take flight,
While I attempt to catch it, and I'm quite the sight!

Sand in my shoes, the price I must pay,
Yet somehow it feels like a game we can play.
The cooler's gone rogue, rolling away with glee,
But I'll chase it down, just you wait and see!

Surf's up, they shout, as I forget how to stand,
Face-first in the surf, oh isn't it grand?
With laughter all around, I emerge from the brine,
A fish out of water, but I don't really mind!

So here's to the giggles, the splashes, the fun,
Where the only competition is how to outrun.
Let the whispers of the waves make us carefree,
In this carnival of waves, just you and me!

Emotions Lost in the Sea Spray

Caught in reverie with salt on my cheeks,
A wave crashes in, oh the slap in my beak!
My beach umbrella flips, like a flying kite,
While I wrestle with sand, what a glorious fight!

Life's a piñata, just a swing and a hit,
With coconuts bouncing and monkeys that twit.
Oh, the sun's blazing down as I sip my cold drink,
But I'm lost in the tangles—oh what do I think?

With squishy flip-flops, I meander away,
Falling for seashells that led me astray.
The tide pulls me under, a swirl and a whirl,
And I giggle aloud as I twist and I twirl!

So toast to these moments, so vivid and bright,
Being silly and giddy, we dance through the light.
With laughter as buoyance, we drift ever free,
In the heart of the moment, just you and me!

Fragrant Hues of Love's Voyage

In a boat made of dreams and a fishy scent,
We paddle through skies, giggling at rent.
With jellyfish hats and sunglasses askew,
Our love's like a picnic with too much fondue.

We toast with coconuts, the drinks spill with cheer,
As monkeys in tuxedos join in with a cheer.
A seagull steals fries, it's a snack-stealing spree,
But we laugh it off, who needs fries, just we?

The sunset's a canvas, hues of lemon and lime,
We paint our adventures, one splash at a time.
With marshmallows as clouds, we float on the sea,
Life's just a carnival; come join in with me!

So grab all your giggles and wear them like flair,
For love's a big party, there's joy everywhere.
We'll dance with the waves 'til the moon takes a peek,
And we'll laugh till we cry, oh, isn't that sleek?

The Surf's Sweet Serenade

The waves sing a tune, can you hear them at play?
They crash in a rhythm, both wild and cliché.
With sandcastles crumbling, oh my, what a sight,
Our shovels are weapons in this childhood fight.

We leap like dolphins, our splashes abound,
While starfish cheer loudly from their spots on the ground.

A crab in a top hat takes tickets for fun,
As we race with the tide—oh, who's won? Nobody won!

The sun sets like a trumpet, blowing kisses galore,
We belt out our laughter, who could ask for more?
With flip-flops as instruments, we march down the shore,
It's a concert of joy, no need to keep score.

As night blankets softly, we gather with glee,
Telling tales of our frolics as bright as can be.
With shadows for partners, we twirl and we sway,
The surf's sweet serenade will never fade away.

Twilight's Breath

As twilight dances on the tip of the night,
We chase the last guppies—what a silly sight!
With fireflies buzzing, we wear them like hats,
Befriending the critters—those cheeky little brats.

The stars start to giggle, they wink with delight,
We sing silly songs 'til we lose track of light.
A crab plays the accordion, oh what a sound!
As we jig through the twilight, our joy knows no bound.

Our shadows stretch long like a cartoonish spree,
We dance with the ocean, it's just you and me.
With marshmallow fluff clouds and a sprinkle of fun,
Twilight's breath wraps us tight, our laughter weighs a ton.

So here's to the moments, the quirky and bright,
With twilight's embrace, every heart feels light.
Let's prance through the silly and chase off the gloom,
As night holds our secrets, let laughter resume!

Oaths Whispered to the Horizon

In flip-flops we solemnly vow to be free,
As seagulls provide the soundtrack for glee.
With picnics of jellybeans, sweet as can be,
We pledge to each other, 'Just look, you and me!'

The horizon smiles back, a wise old friend,
As we promise our laughter will never see end.
With each goofy shimmy, we sketch out our fate,
A confetti of twirls, oh why should we wait?

Our oaths are like bubbles, they pop with a cheer,
For each silly moment is precious and dear.
The ocean, our witness, it grumbles with care,
As we write our own story in sunshine and air.

So here in this moment, we honor the jest,
With hearty agreements, we both feel so blessed.
As the stars start to twinkle and the tide pulls away,
Let's keep laughing together, come what may!

Following the Wind's Song

The seagulls squawk, a raucous choir,
Chasing their dreams, on wings of desire.
Tangled in seaweed, a fish gives a shout,
"I'm more than a snack! Come check me out!"

A crab in a tux, sharp as can be,
Dances on sand like he's fancy-free.
A dolphin dips low with a flip of the tail,
"Catch me if you can!"—and he seems to hail.

The waves play tag, splashing with glee,
While sunburnt tourists sip too much tea.
The beach ball bounces, but not in a line,
My folks scramble, just trying to dine!

The breeze tells jokes, as it rustles the trees,
But all I can think of is getting some cheese.
So here's to the laughter, let's raise a toast,
To salty adventures we love the most!

A Journey in Salt and Stars

The night is a canvas, with stars like sprinkles,
We sail on a boat while the sea gently twinkles.
The fish wear sunglasses, deep under the tide,
As they judge our dance moves, no need to hide!

The moon winks at us, its glow like bright cheese,
A mermaid joins in, she moves with such ease.
Her tail's all a-flash, she twirls and she spins,
"Care to join me, boys? Let's dive in for wins!"

And the waves start to laugh, it's a symphony sweet,
Crashing on shores, offering us a treat.
We start tossing shells just to see how they fly,
But end up with sand crabs, oh my, oh my!

So here's to our journeys through salt and through stars,
Where laughter outshines any fancy cars.
With every new tide, there's fun to be sought,
In night's merry glow, with silliness caught!

Reflections Under the Bay Breeze

Under the palms, where the shadows play,
A squirrel holds court, rights to the bay.
He's donned a fresh scarf, his style's all the rage,
Declaring a meeting! In our beach front page!

The tides giggle softly, tickling the shore,
As we argue over who can snack more.
A sandwich is dropped, and like a great heist,
A flock of lost seagulls swarm, oh how nice!

We trade our best tales, of splashes and slips,
While the fish start to plot our missed lunch trips.
The sun picks a winner, glittering neat,
Whose story was best? The one with the feet!

So here by the bay, under bright dancing leaves,
We chuckle and giggle, we've got such good thieves.
With feathers and laughter, our hearts stay at peace,
In reflections of fun, let the joy never cease!

Beyond the Horizon's Heartbeat

In a boat that's too small, we venture afar,
With fishing rods ready, our dreams are bizarre.
The fish look at us, then burst into giggles,
We cast out our lines, all set for the wiggles!

The sun's a big ball of silly, like clay,
As it melts on the waves, then rolls away.
The dolphins tease us, they leap with such flair,
And we shout from the boat, with sunscreen in hair!

Our snacks fly away with a gust of delight,
As gulls launch a raid, they're hungry tonight.
We wave them goodbye, as they flap and they flap,
While dreaming of dinner and taking a nap.

So we'll sail on forever, with stories so grand,
Beyond the horizon, make funny a brand.
With laughter like waves, splashing high in the air,
Adventure awaits, who wouldn't dare!

Gentle Caress of the Sea

The ocean waves tickle my toes,
As I dodge a fish with a comical pose.
Crabs scuttle past, looking so sly,
I laugh as I chase them, oh me, oh my!

Seagulls squawk loudly, a raucous crew,
Snatching my sandwich, it's true, it's true!
They glide on the wind, the crafty things,
While I wave my arms like I'm sprouting wings.

A jellyfish floats, oh what a sight,
Wobbling and jiggling, what a delight!
I fear for my toes, in a wiggly fray,
But it dances away, what a funny display!

With each splash that tickles my chin,
I grin at the antics the sea life spin.
Nature's a comedian, all in good cheer,
A laugh in the sun, with my friends near here.

Dance of Palms and Dreams

The palms sway and skip in the afternoon sun,
Pretending to dance, oh, what a fun run!
They whisper sweet secrets to the bright sky,
While I try to join them, my feet feel shy.

Each rustle of leaves, a giggling sound,
A riot of nature, where joy is profound.
I spin in a circle, lose track of the beat,
While a lizard just laughs, as if I'm a treat!

In the shade, the shadows play hide-and-seek,
With a kooky old crab that looks quite unique.
I share my deep hopes with a butterfly,
And it flutters away, I guess I'm too sly!

Laughter rolls in like a soft summer breeze,
While I'm wrapped in the warmth, and I giggle with ease.
The dance goes on, with a twist and a twirl,
It's a playful affair in this tropical whirl!

Love Songs under the Canopy

Beneath the green curtain, where sunlight beams,
A squirrel sings love songs, or so it seems.
His tail waves high, like he's got a flare,
While I hum along, catching curious stares.

They say a tree has ears, so I start to confide,
To a sloth hanging out, taking things in stride.
"Hey buddy, what's love?" I jokingly cry,
He blinks and responds with a slow, lazy sigh.

A parrot joins in with a squawk and a wink,
Fluffing his feathers, he's ready to sync.
Together we serenade the soft afternoon,
With nutty old tales and a makeshift tune.

The branches sway gently, holding our dreams,
As critters chuckle softly, or so it seems.
We laugh in our song, under leafy embrace,
In this silly duet, we find our own space.

Echoes of the Shoreline

Footprints mark sand, a trail of delight,
As I wobble and trip, trying to take flight.
The shells play a tune like a playful chart,
With each little pop, it tickles my heart.

The waves joke around, they tease and they splash,
I brace for a wave, then get hit like a crash.
Friends laugh nearby, some wobbling too,
While I bubble with giggles, what else can I do?

A starfish simply grins, sitting so proud,
Watching our antics, he's part of the crowd.
The seagulls they cackle, providing the score,
To the silly little dance on the sunlit shore.

As sunsets paint gold, we all come alive,
With jokes and with stories, our spirits will thrive.
So here we will gather, with laughter galore,
In this grand celebration, we all will explore!

www.ingramcontent.com/pod-product-compliance
Lightning Source LLC
Chambersburg PA
CBHW072125070526
44585CB00016B/1554